I

weblinks

You don't need a computer to use this book. But, for readers who do have access to the Internet, the book provides links to recommended websites which offer additional information and resources on the subject.

You will find weblinks boxes like this on some pages of the book.

---

weblinks

For more information about Islam, go to
www.waylinks.co.uk/
series/21stcentury/Islam

---

waylinks.co.uk

To help you find the recommended websites easily and quickly, weblinks are provided on our own website, **waylinks.co.uk**. These take you straight to the relevant websites and save you typing in the Internet address yourself.

Internet safety

↗ Never give out personal details, which include: your name, address, school, telephone number, email address, password and mobile number.

↗ Do not respond to messages which make you feel uncomfortable – tell an adult.

↗ Do not arrange to meet in person someone you have met on the Internet.

↗ Never send your picture or anything else to an online friend without a parent's or teacher's permission.

↗ If you see anything that worries you, tell an adult.

A note to adults
Internet use by children should be supervised. We recommend that you install filtering software which blocks unsuitable material.

Website content

The weblinks for this book are checked and updated regularly. However, because of the nature of the Internet, the content of a website may change at any time, or a website may close down without notice. While the Publishers regret any inconvenience this may cause readers, they cannot be responsible for the content of any website other than their own.

HODDER
Wayland

21st Century
Islam

David Self

HODDER
Wayland

an imprint of Hodder Children's Books

First published in 2005 by Hodder Wayland,
an imprint of Hodder Children's Books

© Hodder Wayland 2005

Consultant: Dr Fatma Amer, The London Central Mosque
Project Editor, Hodder Wayland: Kirsty Hamilton
Editor: Nicola Barber
Designer: Janet McCallum
Picture Researcher: Shelley Noronha, Glass Onion Pictures
Maps and artwork: Peter Bull

British Library Cataloguing Publication Data
Self, David
Islam – (21st century religions)
1. Islam – Juvenile literature
I. Title
297

ISBN 0750247037

Colour Reproduction by Dot Gradations Ltd, UK
Printed in China

Hodder Children's Books
A division of Hodder Headline Limited
338 Euston Road, London NW1 3BH

The author acknowledges the help of Abdul Majid Jawad in
the writing of the text of this book

The publisher would like to thank the following for permission
to reproduce their pictures: The Art Archive /Turkish and
Islamic Art Museum Istanbul/Harper Collins Publishers 8,
Dagli Orti 31; Bridgeman Art Library
www.bridgeman.co.uk/University Library, Istanbul, Turkey 38;
Corbis/SUPRI/Reuters 44; Hutchison Picture Library 29;
Impact Photos 4; Alex Keene 26; Ann and Bury Peerless 12,
39, 41; Peter Sanders Photography Ltd 6, 7, 9, 18, 19, 20, 23,
24, 28, 30, 32, 34, 35, 36, 37, 40; Topfoto 11, 13, 14, 15, 16,
17, 21, 22, 25, 33, 42, 43, 45

Contents

Note

When Muslims use the name of their Prophet, they usually follow it with the blessing 'Peace be upon him' – shown in Arabic as: The Prophet Muhammad ﷺ

In the Western world years are numbered as either BC *('Before Christ') or* AD *(Anno Domini – which is Latin for 'In the year of our Lord...'). In this book, the more neutral terms* BCE *('Before the Common Era') and* CE *('Common Era') are used. The Muslim calendar counts years from the date on which the Prophet and his companions left Makkah for Madinah. Its years are numbered* AH *('After the Hijrah').*

Introduction

For Muslims, the followers of the religion Islam, the most important teacher in the world is the Prophet Muhammad ﷺ. For them, the Prophet Muhammad ﷺ is the last and the greatest of the prophets of God.

One God

Muhammad ﷺ worked as a trader in the city of Makkah (also known as Mecca), in what is now Saudi Arabia. An angel appeared to him several times, giving him messages which he was to repeat to the people of Makkah. These messages were later collected together to form the Muslim holy book, the Qur'an. Muslims believe the Qur'an is the word of God, written in its own style of Arabic. Because it is the word of God, it is always treated with great respect.

The most important message, or teaching, of the angel was that there is only one God, whose name is God – or, in Arabic, 'Allah'.

Islam

The teaching that the Prophet Muhammad ﷺ brought to his people is not named after him, but is known as Islam, which means 'peace and submission' (or 'obedience to God'). Nor are the followers of Islam named after him: they are called Muslims.

For Muslims, the Prophet did not start a new religion. He taught the same message as the other prophets of God who had lived before him including Noah, Ibrahim (Abraham), Musa (Moses) and Isa (Jesus): that there is one and only one true God. In Arabic, this teaching is called *tawhid*.

Islam worldwide

Islam is now the second largest religion in the world, with about 1,300 million Muslims living in almost every country worldwide.

weblinks

For more information about Islam, go to
www.waylinks.co.uk/series/21stcentury/Islam

◄ *In desert countries, people often travel in the cool of the night. The stars are their guide and the moon is their light – so a star and the crescent moon form the symbol of Islam, seen here on a building in the Maldives.*

In more than fifty countries, there are more Muslims than followers of any other religion. These countries stretch from Morocco in the west across North Africa to the Middle East, and east to Afghanistan and Pakistan. There are also many Muslims in central Africa, as well as in Indonesia, China and Russia. Many Muslims have settled in European countries – for example, there are about 1.5 million Muslims living in Britain.

For 800 years, the Muslim people led the world in providing education and in the development of science. But from the 18th century CE onwards, many Muslim countries came under Western control, some being conquered by European armies and then ruled as part of Western empires. In the last sixty years, most of these countries have regained their independence and Muslims are now keen to preserve their own ways of life, based on the Qur'an and the teachings of the Prophet Muhammad ﷺ.

Countries with the largest Muslim populations

Country	Approximate number of Muslims
Indonesia	170,310,000
Pakistan	136,000,000
Bangladesh	106,050,000
India	103,000,000
Turkey	62,410,000
Iran	60,790,000
Egypt	53,730,000
Nigeria	47,720,000
China	37,108,000

▼ This map shows the worldwide spread of Islam today.

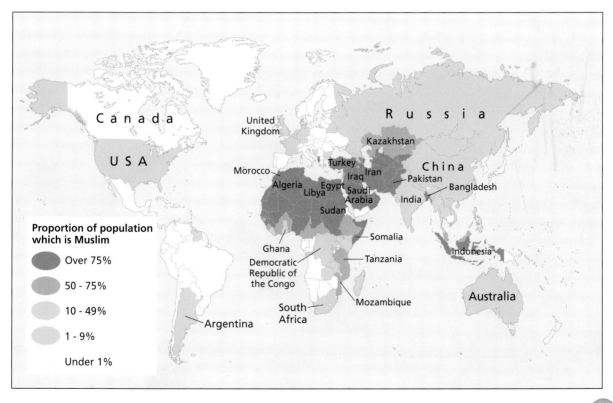

Proportion of population which is Muslim

- Over 75%
- 50 - 75%
- 10 - 49%
- 1 - 9%
- Under 1%

1* The growth of Islam

Islam is one of the great religions of the world. It teaches that there is only one God – a God who has made everything, knows everything and sees everything. As Muslims say, 'There is no God but Allah'.

The Prophet of Islam

Muhammad ﷺ lived in the city of Makkah in what is now Saudi Arabia from the year 570CE until 632. His father died before his birth and his mother died when he was six, so he was looked after by his grandfather and later by an uncle. His family was quite poor and, like most people at that time, he was not taught either to read or write. When he grew up, he worked for his uncle who was a trader in the city.

Later, Muhammad ﷺ worked for a wealthy widow called Khadijah, who also lived in Makkah, caring for her trade. Eventually Khadijah proposed marriage to him. Muhammad ﷺ accepted, and Khadijah went on to bear him six children.

▼ The Great Mosque of Makkah, showing the black, cube-shaped Ka'bah in its courtyard (see page 9), and the modern city beyond its walls.

Mount Hira

At that time, the people of Makkah had forgotten their earlier belief in the one God and were leading immoral lives. There was much fighting, drinking and poverty. Instead of worshipping God, many people worshipped statues or idols made of stone or wood. Although Muhammad ﷺ was happy and content with his own life, he became increasingly concerned about the social injustices he saw in Makkah. He felt the need to be close to God and he would often walk north out of Makkah to a hill called Mount Hira. There he sat in a hillside cave. As he watched the stars and the moon, it is said he came to know the greatness of God.

The Angel Jibril

One night, when Muhammad ﷺ was in the cave, he heard a voice. In front of him he saw a holy spirit, the Angel Jibril (also known as Gabriel).
"Recite" said the angel.
"What should I recite?" asked Muhammad ﷺ.
"Recite in the name of God." Muhammad ﷺ repeated the words the angel spoke to him until he knew them by heart.

Ten months later, the angel appeared to him again.
"Warn the people. Tell them they must worship and praise the one God and give up their

wicked ways." After that, the Angel Jibril appeared often to Muhammad ﷺ, giving him many more revelations (messages) which he was to teach to the people of Makkah – especially the message that there is only one God, whose name is Allah.

From then on, Muhammad ﷺ was known as the Prophet and Messenger of God and all the angel told him was preserved in the Qur'an, which is treasured by all Muslims as the word of God.

➤ It is in this cave in the rock face of Mount Hira that the Prophet is said to have prayed before being visited by the Angel Jibril.

Makkah

Some time after the Angel Jibril had revealed the teaching of the Qur'an to the Prophet, he started to teach the people of Makkah what had been told to him. Many listened and became followers of these teachings, the way of Islam.

There were, however, many people in Makkah who did not welcome the Prophet's new message about the One God. These people worshipped idols and other gods. They thought that if Muhammad ﷺ persuaded everyone that their idols were worthless and had them destroyed, nobody would visit the city and their businesses would be ruined. The rulers of Makkah tried to starve the Prophet and his family to death by cutting off all his sources of food. When that failed, they tried to stop people trading with his family. That also failed. After two years, they decided to kill Muhammad ﷺ while he slept.

The spider's web

Muslims believe that God warned the Prophet in a vision of what was about to happen. Under the cover of darkness, Muhammad ﷺ and his faithful friend and servant, Abu Bakr, managed to escape. Travelling south, they eventually reached some mountains where they found a cave in which to hide.

The Prophet's enemies followed the fugitives to the mountains. Inside the cave, the Prophet and Abu Bakr heard their enemies approaching. Outside, the trackers found the mouth of the cave. But one of the trackers pointed to a spider's web that covered its entrance. Above it, a branch hung low, weighed down by a grey dove which was singing gently. The pursuers moved on, believing that nobody had entered that cave for months.

Al Hijrah

Eventually the Prophet and Abu Bakr made the difficult journey across the desert to a place called Yathrib, which became known as the city of al-Madinah. They were welcomed by the people, and the Prophet taught his message in safety. It was in Madinah that the first mosque was built.

Eight years later, in the year 630CE, the Prophet was able to return in triumph to Makkah where the people accepted Islam as their religion. All the idols were removed from a holy place called the Ka'bah, which Muslims believe was the first house built on earth for the worship of the one God.

The Muslim calendar dates from the departure of the Prophet from Makkah (16 July 622CE) on his journey to Madinah. The event is celebrated annually as *Al Hijrah* which means 'the journey' or 'migration', and is the first day of the Muslim year.

The Ka'bah

The Ka'bah is a building in the shape of a cube; twelve metres long, ten metres wide and fifteen metres high (the word Ka'bah means 'cube'). Muslims believe the first Ka'bah was built by the first man, Adam, after he had been sent away from the Garden of Eden, as a house in which to praise God. Later, a man Muslims call Ibrahim (and whom Jews and Christians call Abraham) built a new Ka'bah in the same place. This Ka'bah was kept holy for many years – but was then used for pagan worship until the Prophet Muhammad ﷺ once again made it a place for worship to the One God. (See page 30 for more about the Ka'bah.)

➤ Pilgrims in their white robes surround the Ka'bah.

◄ This is a Muslim artist's representation of the building of the Prophet's house, which was also the first mosque, in Madinah. The painting dates from the 18th century.

The Muslim calendar

Islamic years are counted from the Hijrah (AH means 'After the Hijrah'), which occurred on 16 July 622CE. There are roughly 103 Muslim (lunar) years to every 100 Western (solar) years (see page 27). Common Era years (that is, years AD) can be calculated using this formula:

CE year = AH year + 622 – (AH year ÷ 33).

To calculate Islamic years from CE years use this formula:

$$\text{AH year} = \text{CE year} - 622 + \frac{\text{CE year} - 622}{32}$$

The four khalifahs

The Prophet Muhammad ﷺ died in 632CE. After his death, his close friend and son-in-law Abu Bakr became the chosen leader of the Muslims and successor to the Prophet. The Arabic word for successor is 'khalifah' (sometimes spelt caliph). A good and kind man, Abu Bakr ruled for two years until his own death. He was followed by a clever political leader and military general called Umar, who ruled for ten years until he was murdered in 644CE.

Before his death, Umar set up a council that would choose the next khalifah. The council suggested two men, Uthman bin Affan and Ali bin Talib, both sons-in-law of the Prophet. Eventually Uthman (who was a gentle and a generous man) was elected by the elders of the people as the third khalifah. He ruled for ten years until his assassination in 656CE.

Ali, who was the Prophet's cousin as well as his son-in-law, became the fourth khalifah. He proved to be a brave but humble leader and his many speeches, sermons and letters are highly regarded. But then in 661CE, he too was murdered.

These first four khalifahs are known as the *rashidun*, or 'rightly guided'; that is, they were seen as God's representatives on earth. In later centuries, the word khalifah or caliph was also used to mean an (unelected) leader or emperor.

The spread of Islam

Within one hundred years of the death of the Prophet, Islam had spread far beyond the Arabian peninsula. The Muslim armies first marched into nearby countries and then moved rapidly on, conquering as they went. The armies were followed by traders and teachers of the faith. By the year 732CE, Muslims ruled from Spain to India, including southern France, all of northern Africa, Egypt, Arabia and what are now Iraq and Iran. Although there were different rulers in different areas, all were united by the Arabic language and laws based on the Qur'an.

SPAIN

Mediterranean Sea

•Baghdad
Damascus

NORTH AFRICA

Red Sea

ARABIA

•Makkah

INDIA

Arabian Sea

Arabia at the time of Muhammad

Conquests during the time of the four Khalifahs

Conquests by 732CE

Non-Muslim countries

◄ This map shows the rapid spread of Islam after the death of the Prophet. By the time of Umar, Muslims ruled from Libya in the west to Afghanistan in the east, as well as what became known as Arabia.

Shi'ah and Sunni

Following the death of the Prophet there were people who opposed his successors, and who wanted Ali (see page 10) to be khalifah instead. Those who supported Ali wanted all future leaders to come from the Prophet's family. These supporters became known as the Shi'at-Ali, which means 'the party of Ali'. They continued to be a strong group within Islam and today they are known as Shi'ah Muslims. Many Shi'ahs believe it is right to fight for what they believe, even if it means being killed themselves. They live mainly in Iran and southern Iraq.

About 90 per cent of Muslims belong to a group called the Sunnis, who take their name from the Sunnah (see page 19), the 'way of the Prophet'. Like the Shi'ahs, Sunni Muslims follow the teachings of the Prophet and believe that the Qur'an shows them the way to live. They respect Muslim teachers called imams but, unlike the Shi'ahs, the Sunnis do not have any special clergy or priests. Shi'ahs believe there were twelve imams who had special powers, the first imam being Ali, the fourth khalifah. They are now led by teachers called ayatollahs, and have other clergy and teachers who explain hidden meanings in the Qur'an.

➤ Although most Muslims in Pakistan are Sunnis, there are many Shi'ahs. Here they carry black flags at the festival of Ashura (see pages 26 and 27), in memory of the martyrdom of al-Husain ibn Ali, son of the fourth khalifah, Ali.

Jerusalem

Conflict and suspicion between the Islamic countries and the Christian (Western) world dates from early times. In particular, there were bitter quarrels about the city of Jerusalem, a holy city for both Jews and Christians as well Muslims. Jerusalem was captured by the second khalifah, Umar, in 638CE. On entering the city, Umar treated all the people well, and it is said that nobody was harmed. Much later, in 1099, Christian armies laid siege to the city, eventually capturing it back from Muslim control. It is said that the Christians killed 70,000 people during this 'crusade'.

The Muslims re-captured the city once again in 1187. Their leader Salah-ad-Din (sometimes known as Saladin) ordered that no Christian should be harmed and he made peace with King Richard I of England. Nevertheless, the crusades continued throughout the 13th and 14th centuries, as Christian armies tried to take Jerusalem back under their control.

➤ *The Dome of the Rock (Qubbat al-Sakhra) in Jerusalem is built on the spot from which the Prophet is said to have been taken on a 'Night Journey' to heaven by the Angel Jibril, as recorded in the Hadith (see page 19).*

Powerful empires

All this time, the Muslim world prospered and gained in power and wealth. Many Islamic empires were established, including the mighty Ottoman Empire which lasted from about 1300 to 1920. Based in what is now Turkey, at one time it stretched from Algeria in Africa to Basra in Iraq, and north to include Hungary and parts of Russia. Its greatest ruler was Emperor Suleiman, who held power in the 16th century. His palaces in the Ottoman capital, Istanbul, so dazzled Western visitors that they called him Suleiman the Magnificent. At about the same time, another powerful Muslim empire, that of the Mughals, stretched across India.

The Muslim rulers of these great empires were not Arabs: the Mughal rulers claimed descent from warlike tribes in Mongolia while the Ottoman rulers were Turks. In both empires, the discovery of gunpowder was used to gain and keep power, and the imperial courts were centres of splendour, vast wealth, luxury and learning.

The Mughals

The mighty Mughal Empire was founded by Babur in 1526. Babur became ruler of Turkestan when he was twelve and later conquered Afghanistan. In 1525 he invaded India and conquered large areas of the country over the next two years. Babur's grandson, Akbar (ruled 1556-1605), doubled the size of the area under Mughal control, so that the Mughal Empire stretched across almost all of what is now India and Pakistan. Akbar built great palaces at Delhi and Agra. The Mughal Empire was attacked by the Persians (now Iranians) in 1739 and during the 19th century the British gradually took control of the country, bringing the Mughal Empire to an end in 1858.

➤ *This painting of the Mughal court shows two Christian priests visiting the Emperor Akbar. It is from the Akbar-nama, a chronicle of Akbar's reign completed in the late 16th century.*

Ruled by the West

For 250 years, from about 1700 to 1950, large parts of the Muslim world came under Western rule. It was in 1857, for example, that what had been the great Muslim city of Delhi in India was captured by the British.

Many Muslim countries became colonies in empires ruled from Britain, France and the Netherlands. In Indonesia, the Dutch did not allow local people to go to secondary school. In Tunisia, the French created laws that made traditional Muslim medicine against the law. In some places, Islamic libraries were destroyed, and treasures were removed and taken back to Western cities.

New movements

Some Muslims said that the end of the Muslim empires was largely the fault of the Muslims themselves. They suggested that some Muslim emperors had become corrupt and too fond of luxury for themselves, and that these rulers had neglected the poor in their own empires. They also said that there had been too many arguments and divisions between Muslim leaders, and that religious scholars keen to preserve their own power had prevented new ideas from spreading.

Many Muslims began to emphasize the need to re-visit the teachings of the Qur'an and to live them in their purest form. In the 20th century, the result of this new emphasis was the start of many Muslim reformation movements, beginning in Arabia where, in 1926, the Islamic kingdom of Saudi Arabia came into being. Since the end of the Second World War (in 1945), Muslim countries have regained their independence. For example, in 1947, British rule came to a violent end in India as the country was partitioned, or divided, into two separate countries. In the northwest, the independent state of Pakistan was set up in a region where mainly Muslim people had lived. The larger area, which was mainly Hindu, kept the name of India.

◄ *These oilfields in Kuwait supply fuel to the Western world. It was the invasion of this area by President Saddam of Iraq in 1990 that caused the First Gulf War.*

The discovery of oil has brought new wealth to some Muslim countries, particularly in the Middle East. At the same time, people in some of these countries have turned against Western values, and are trying to lead their lives independently and in a way that they feel is faithful to the teachings revealed by the Prophet.

Sufis

Since the early days of Islam, there have been Muslims who have tried to become as close to God as possible by leading a very simple way of life. Such people became known as Sufis because they wore long woollen robes, called sufs, *of the kind said to be worn by the Prophet Muhammad ﷺ when he visited the cave at Hira. Sufis use techniques such as chanting or performing rhythmic, whirling dances to try to achieve a closeness with God.*

▼ *Those Sufis who perform whirling dances have sometimes been known as 'whirling dervishes'. The Arabic word 'dervish' means a 'member of a religious group'.*

Muslim beliefs and teachings

For all Muslims, faith is built upon the Qur'an. The Qur'an tells Muslims what they should believe and how they should live their lives. Muslims believe that the Qur'an was not written by the Prophet but is God's own word, and therefore should always be treated with great respect.

The Qur'an

The Prophet Muhammad ﷺ could neither read nor write. Each time the Angel Jibril revealed more of God's teachings to him on Mount Hira, Muhammad ﷺ learned them by heart. Back in Makkah, he repeated them to his friends who also learned them by heart and wrote them down in various places and on any materials that came to hand – parchment, leather, even pieces of bone. After the Prophet had arrived in Madinah, the Angel Jibril revealed more teachings to him.

▼ *These two pages from a 17th-century Qur'an are beautifully decorated with patterns and geometric designs. The Qur'an is never illustrated with pictures of living beings (see page 39).*

Translating the Qur'an

The Qur'an is not written in 'everyday' Arabic but in its own style. When Muslims go to the mosque, they hear it read in this form of Arabic. Nowadays millions of Muslims do not speak Arabic, and even modern Arabic speakers do not always understand the Arabic of the Qur'an. For them, the Qur'an may be translated into their own language – but Muslims believe that no translation can ever convey exactly what the original means.

Arabic letters are very different from Western ones. Sometimes, different English spellings are used to imitate the sound of an Arabic word – which is why the word 'Qur'an' is sometimes spelt 'Koran' in English.

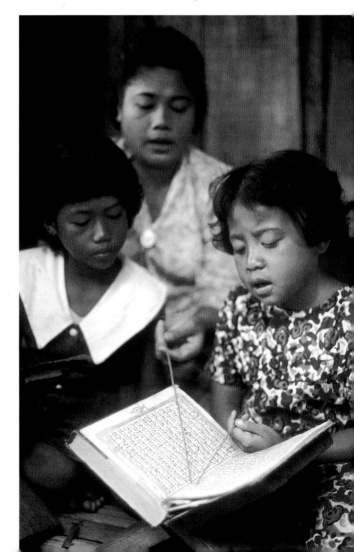

▼ *Young Muslim girls in the Philippines learn to recite sections of the Qur'an by heart.*

After his death, the Prophet's closest friend Abu Bakr wanted to keep all the teachings safe, but it was the third khalifah, Uthman, who eventually ordered a man called Zaid ibn Thabit and a team of scribes to collect all that had been revealed. The sayings were written down exactly as the Prophet had dictated them, to form the Qur'an. Ever since then, the words of the Qur'an, whether written or printed, have remained unchanged. The term 'Qur'an' is Arabic for 'recitation' – because of the angel's first word ('Recite') to the Prophet (see page 7).

The Qur'an contains 114 chapters which are called *surahs*. Each surah (except surah 9) begins with the words: 'In the name of Allah, the compassionate, the merciful.' These words are called the *Bismillah*. Muslims say the Bismillah before eating or doing any important job as a way of asking God's blessing. It is said that the Bismillah was written on the wings of the Angel Jibril. The book itself is treated with great respect and must only be touched with clean hands and never while eating or drinking. Nor must it ever touch the ground.

The teachings of Islam

Muslims respect the holy books of the Jewish religion and the Christian Gospels, but they believe that the Qur'an is God's final and complete teaching for his people. It is not a book of stories about ancient times – it is a book of teachings, laws and wise sayings. It is written in a mixture of rhythmic prose and poetry, and its 114 chapters or surahs are always arranged in the same order. It is said that the Angel Jibril told the Prophet that they should be arranged in this way.

The shorter surahs were mostly revealed in Makkah, before the Muslims' migration to Madinah. Nearly all of what was revealed in Makkah teaches Muslims about the oneness of God, about creation and life after death. These surahs also speak of the greatness and mercy of God.

▼ *In accordance with Muslim tradition, these young women students at the Yusuf Islam School in London are wearing headscarves and modest dress.*

As a result of the Angel Jibril's instruction, the longer surahs come at the beginning of the Qur'an. These longer surahs, were revealed in Madinah after the migration and the establishment of the first Muslim state. That is why they tell Muslims how to live their lives based on equality and social justice. They include laws about how to run the state, as well as instructions to dress modestly and not to be greedy. There are rules forbidding Muslims to charge or to pay interest on money that they lend or borrow, and there are instructions to those who act as judges that they should always be merciful.

The Sirah

It is said that everything the Prophet Muhammad ﷺ did was written down so that Muslims know how he spoke, slept, dressed and walked. They know about his behaviour as a husband and a father, and how he treated women, children and animals. All this is called the *Sirah*.

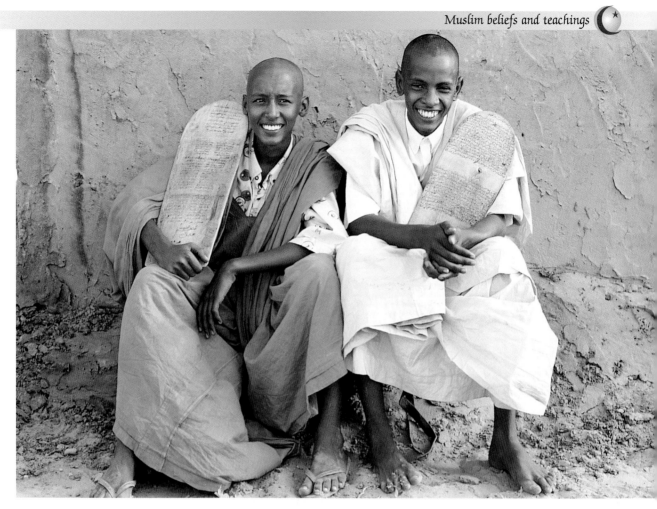

▲ *Two Muslim boys at Qur'an School in the Islamic Republic of Mauritania, in western Africa. Even though they speak a dialect called Hansaniya Arabic, they learn the extracts from the Qur'an on their tablets in traditional Arabic.*

The Hadith

Some years after the death of the Prophet, all his sayings were collected together. Scholars had strict rules for deciding which sayings were to be included, and those sayings that were agreed as being genuine were called the *Hadith*. The word means 'statement'.

The Sunnah

Together, the Sirah and the Hadith are called the Sunnah. The word means 'method' or 'example'. Muslims try to live their lives in the way shown by the Qur'an and the Sunnah.

Some sayings of the Prophet

'The world is green and beautiful and God has made you his steward over it.'

'When you go to visit the sick, comfort them in their grief by saying "You will get well and live long."'

'God does not look upon your bodies and appearances. He looks upon your hearts and deeds.'

'God is gentle and loves gentleness in all things.'

The Shahadah

Muslims all around the world learn that the first duty of Islam is to make a statement of their faith. This is done by saying the *Shahadah*:

'There is no god but God and Muhammad is his Prophet.'

In Arabic it is:

'La ila' ha illallah Muhammad ur rasulullah.'

It is by saying this (and believing it) that a person becomes a Muslim.

Although Muslims honour and respect other prophets such as Musa (Moses) and Isa (Jesus), they do not believe that Isa was divine (that he was the son of God) even though they do believe in his virgin birth. They believe that with Muhammad ﷺ, God completed the revelation of his truth, a revelation that had begun with the earlier prophets or messengers.

Learning the Qur'an

Muslims believe that the Qur'an is the most important book in the world, and many Muslims learn large sections of the Qur'an by heart, especially when they are young. Schools in many Muslim countries make this a part of the curriculum. In non-Muslim countries, children often go to special classes (sometimes called 'mosque school') after their ordinary school day has finished. In these classes they are taught by the local imam to recite sections of the Qur'an. The language and the rhythms in which it is written make it easier to learn by heart.

A number of Muslims learn to recite the whole Qur'an. Anyone who achieves this is much respected and is allowed to use the title *hafiz* as part of their name. It is estimated that there are several million people alive at any one time who are hafiz.

▼ *Like all Arabic, the Shahadah is read from right to left.*

The 'Five Pillars' of Islam

Islam has five rules or 'pillars'. They are called pillars because they help a Muslim to live a good life – in the same way that pillars support a building. They are mentioned throughout the Qur'an:

1 *Shahadah or making a statement of faith.*

2 *Salah or prayer (see pages 22-3)*

3 *Zakah or helping the needy (see pages 36-7)*

4 *Sawm or fasting (see page 28)*

5 *Hajj or pilgrimage (see pages 30-1)*

Other rules in the Qur'an teach Muslims always to be honest and generous; never to eat pork or to drink alcohol, and never to gamble or to lend money for profit. Muslims must also be ready to fight to defend their faith.

▼ *Young boys in Karachi, Pakistan, go to a special school to learn to recite the Qur'an.*

Private and public worship

Muslims believe that their whole lives should be lived for God. To be a Muslim is to submit oneself to God, who is merciful and just. Prayer is an act of submission to God.

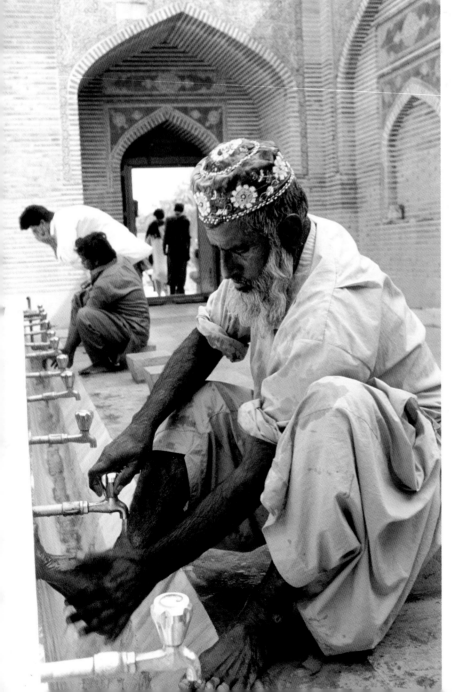

Salah

One of the five duties of Islam is prayer, which is known as salah (or salat). The Muslim holy book, the Qur'an, repeatedly says how important it is to pray – and to pray at set times: 'Prayer at fixed times has been enjoined on the believers.'

Muslims pray five times a day, at the times taught by the Prophet. These five set times are:

- between the first sign of daylight and sunrise
- just after midday
- just after the middle of the afternoon
- after sunset but before dark
- when it is dark.

▼ *A Muslim in Thata, Pakistan, performs the ritual act of wudu before prayer. This involves washing first the face, then the hands and lower arms, before washing the feet.*

These prayers may be said in a mosque or at home, but Muslims can pray anywhere that is clean – provided they have also made themselves clean. This special act of washing before prayer is called *wudu*.

To pray, Muslims must face in the direction of the holy city of Makkah where the Ka'bah is (see page 9). When they are ready, they often put down a prayer mat before they say their prayers – in Arabic.

A different position is taken for each part of the prayer. First, the Muslim stands to show he is listening to God. Then he bows to show respect to God. Next he bows low twice, touching the ground with forehead, knees, nose and palms – showing that he is submitting himself to the will of God. Between each of these low bows, he sits back on his heels. Special words are said at each point, and all the movements are repeated two, three or four times according to the time of day. Muslims also say their own private prayers in their own language.

The Exordium

As part of their prayers, Muslims repeat the opening words of the Qur'an:

*'In the name of God,
The most Gracious,
The most Merciful,
All praise be to God alone, the Lord of Creation,
The most Gracious, the most Merciful King of Judgement Day!
You alone we worship and to You alone we pray for help.
Guide us in the right way – the way of those you have blessed, not the way of those that have been condemned by you or of those who go astray.'
(Surah 1)*

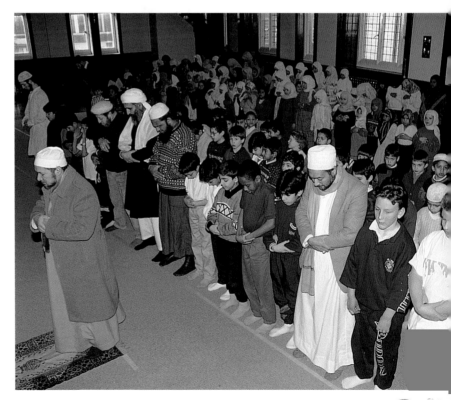

➤ *Muslims join in prayer at the Islamia School in Brent, in north London, UK.*

Going to the mosque

The place where Muslims gather together to worship God is called a mosque. Many mosques have a tall tower called a minaret. Five times a day, at the set times, a man called a *mu'adhin* (sometimes spelt muezzin) traditionally calls Muslims from the minaret to pray to God. The most important prayers of the week are those said after noon on a Friday. At this time, Muslim men go to a mosque to pray together. Women may also go, but many choose to pray at home.

In each mosque, there is a place where Muslims may wash so that they are not dirty in any way when they pray to God. They also take off their shoes before entering a mosque, making sure that the dirty soles of the shoes are not left pointing upwards towards God. There are no chairs or seats in the main prayer hall. Often there are mats on which Muslims can kneel and bow low or 'prostrate' themselves to pray. (The word 'mosque' means 'place for prostration'.)

Wherever they are in the world, Muslims face the holy city of Makkah to pray and so, in each mosque, on one wall is an empty arch (called a *mihrab*) which shows the direction of Makkah (the *qiblah*). The person leading the prayers may stand in front of the mihrab.

Although Muslims can worship anywhere that is clean, the Qur'an says that whenever forty men live in the same area, they should have a mosque. Many mosques are large, very

▼ *The New Federal Mosque in Kuala Lumpur, Malaysia, has (like many large mosques) a huge central courtyard. It has two minarets from which the faithful are called to prayer. It was opened in 2000 and can hold up to 17,000 worshippers at one time. Its design was influenced by traditional Ottoman mosques in Turkey.*

handsome buildings, often with huge domes, but a mosque may simply be a conversion of an ordinary house. There are never any pictures or statues in a mosque. This is because the Prophet Muhammad ﷺ thought people might worship them instead of God. But there are often many beautiful carpets or hangings, decorated with patterns or words from the Qur'an.

Besides the main area (called the Prayer Hall or Room), there may be a separate area where women can pray. There may also be a courtyard and rooms used for teaching and meetings, but there is no obligation on Muslim women to attend the mosque – and most don't. Instead, they fulfil their daily obligations to pray within the home.

The imam

At Friday prayers, there is a sermon or talk. This is usually given by the imam, a leader or teacher chosen by the other Muslims at that mosque because of his wisdom and knowledge of the Qur'an.

➤ *Muslim men attend the Islamic Cultural Center mosque in New York. They sit facing the mihrab (arch) which indicates the qiblah – the direction of Makkah. To the right of the mihrab is the minbar, from where the imam gives his Friday sermon.*

weblinks

For more information about going to the mosque, go to www.waylinks.co.uk/series/21stcentury/Islam

Festivals and holy days

Muslims are required by Islamic law to celebrate at least two festivals: Id-ul-Fitr and Id-ul-Adha ('Id', sometimes spelt 'Eid', means 'festival'; see page 28). But many Muslims celebrate several other special days in each year. The Muslim year is shorter than the Western year (see box), so these annual events in the Muslim calendar happen on different dates in the Western calendar every year.

Al Hijrah (1 Muharram)

This festival, which occurs on New Year's Day in the Islamic calendar, is a reminder of the Hijrah when the Prophet Muhammad ﷺ migrated from Makkah to Madinah. It marks the start of the spread of Islam around the world (see page 8).

Ashura (10 Muharram)

On this day, Shi'ah Muslims remember the martyrdom of al-Husain ibn Ali, a grandson of the Prophet, in 680CE at Karbala in Iraq.

Maulid al-Nabi (The Day of the Prophet; 12 Rabi' al-Awwal)

The 'Day of the Prophet' commemorates both his birth and death.

Laylat-al-Mi'raj (The Night Journey; 27 Rajab)

This festival celebrates the 'Night Journey' made by the Prophet Muhammad ﷺ with the Angel Jibril. They went from Makkah to Jerusalem in a single night on a winged horse. From a place in Jerusalem where the Dome of the Rock now stands, it is said that the Prophet ascended into heaven to meet the earlier prophets and eventually God. On this night the Prophet learned the importance of praying five times a day. Some Muslims believe that this was not an actual journey but a vision.

Ramadan

Ramadan is the month in which Muslims fast each day during the hours of daylight (see pages 28-9).

Laylat-ul-Qadr (The Night of Power; 27 Ramadan)

This festival marks the night in which the Qur'an was first revealed to the Prophet by the Angel Jibril. Many Muslims spend the night reading the Qur'an or praying in their local mosque.

---
weblinks

For more information about Muslim festivals, go to www.waylinks.co.uk/series/21stcentury/Islam

---

◀ *A selection of Id (or Eid) cards which Muslims exchange in celebration of the end of the month of Ramadan.*

The Islamic months

Islam has its own calendar based on the movements of the moon (rather than the movement of the earth around the sun on which the Western calendar is based). This Islamic calendar has twelve months but each is only 29 or 30 days long (the time between one new moon and the next). As a result, Muslim years are usually eleven days shorter than Western years. This means that, each year, Muslim holy days 'move' forwards through the calendar used in Western countries. Islamic months begin at sunset with the first sighting of the new moon in a given area.

Islamic months	Festivals (with date)
Muharram	1 Al Hijrah (Prophet's journey to Madinah)
	10 Ashura
Safar	
Rabi' al-Awwal	12 Maulid al-Nabi (The Day of the Prophet)
(sometimes called Rabi I)	
Rabi' ath-Thani	
(sometimes called Rabi II)	
Jamadi al-Awwal	
(sometimes called Jamadi I or Jumad I)	
Jamadi al-Akhir	
(sometimes called Jamadi II or Jumad II)	
Rajab	27 Laylat-al-Mi'raj (The Night Journey)
Sha'ban	
Ramadan	27 Laylat-ul-Qadr (The Night of Power)
Shawwal	1 Id-ul-Fitr (Day after Ramadan)
Dhul-Qa'da	
Dhul-Hijja	Al Hajj (Pilgrimage to Makkah)
	10 Id-ul-Adha (End of the Hajj)

Id-ul-Fitr (1 Shawwal)

The day after Ramadan is a great celebration. In Islamic countries it is a public holiday. It begins with an early meal. Then everyone puts on their best clothes and goes to the mosque and, later, they visit relatives and friends to swap presents and to give each other sweets. People wish each other "Id Mubarak" ("Blessed be your celebration") and exchange Id cards.

Id-ul-Adha (10 Dhul-Hijja)

This important festival marks the end of the Hajj (see pages 30-1). It is celebrated by all Muslims and not just those who make the pilgrimage. An animal (a sheep, goat, cow or even a camel) is sacrificed, and its meat is shared between the family, friends and the poor. This is done in remembrance of the sacrifice sent by God to Ibrahim (Abraham), to take the place of Ibrahim's son Ismail whom he was about to sacrifice to God.

Ramadan

Ramadan is the ninth month of the Muslim year (see page 27) and is special because it was the month in which the Prophet began to receive the teaching of Islam from the Angel Jibril (see page 7). To remind themselves of this, Muslims fast on each of the thirty days of Ramadan during daylight hours. They don't eat, drink or smoke from dawn until sunset. They also avoid all sexual relations at this time. Fasting (sawm) is one of the five rules or 'pillars' of Islam that Muslims must obey (see page 21).

The month begins with the first sighting of the new moon, so the fast starts at slightly

▲ *A British Muslim family share their evening meal after their daily fast during the month of Ramadan.*

different times in different countries. During this month, Muslims are also meant to say extra prayers and to try to read the whole of the Qur'an. All adult Muslims are expected to keep the fast, but very old people, people who are ill, those making a long journey and women who are pregnant or feeding a baby are excused. So too are young children, but most children try to fast once they reach the age of twelve. Some younger ones will fast for part of the day or on Fridays, Saturdays and Sundays by way of practise. Ramadan is also a time for giving to charity.

During the month of Ramadan, before sunrise Muslims have a meal called *suhoor* consisting of foods such as bread with olive oil, rice or porridge, boiled eggs or dates and other fruit. After sunset, they end that day's fast with *iftar*, a few dates or nuts, savoury pastries and fruit drinks. After evening prayers, they share in the main family meal of the day.

In our own words

"I fast not because food is bad or eating is wicked. I fast because going without food all day makes me really enjoy my evening meal. A meal at the end of the day's fast is something I really look forward to. I also fast to remind me that many people are too poor to eat whenever they feel like it. It makes me think of people who live where there's a shortage of food. Often, we reach for something to nibble the moment we feel the slightest bit hungry. Fasting makes me not give in the moment I feel hungry. It helps make my mind stronger than my body"

Zulfiquar, aged 13, UK

▼ *In Jakarta, Indonesia, Muslims gather for early morning prayers on Id-ul-Fitr, the day after Ramadan.*

The Ka'bah

The fifth duty or pillar of Islam is to make a pilgrimage to Makkah. The word for this duty is 'Hajj'.

The city of Makkah (in what is now Saudi Arabia) is important to Muslims not only because it was the birthplace of the Prophet of Islam, Muhammad ﷺ, but also because it is the site of the Ka'bah. When Muslims make the Hajj, they believe they are following not only in the footsteps of the Prophet but also in those of Adam and of Ibrahim, whom they consider to be their forefathers (see page 4). Today, the Ka'bah stands in the courtyard of the Great Mosque of Makkah. It is covered in a black silk and cotton cloth with the words of the Qur'an embroidered upon it. Inside, the Ka'bah is unfurnished. Ordinary pilgrims do not enter it.

Al Hajj

The Hajj is performed during the second week of the twelfth month of the Muslim year. As the pilgrims approach Makkah, they stop to put on pilgrim dress. For a man, this is two pieces of white, unsewn cloth. Women veil their faces. The purpose of this clothing is to stress simplicity and equality: nobody's wealth or status can be told from their dress.

On entering the courtyard of the Great Mosque, pilgrims walk seven times round the Ka'bah (which they have always faced when saying their prayers back at home). From the Ka'bah they walk briskly between the two small hills of Safa and Marwah which are at a close distance from the Ka'bah within

▼ *During the Hajj, pilgrims live in a vast tented city near Makkah.*

Makkah. This is done in memory of the time when Hagar, mother of Ishmael (said to be an ancestor of all Muslim people) searched in this desert place for water for her baby son. It is said that God caused a spring (called Zam Zam) to gush out of the rocky ground. Pilgrims take home water from the spring to those who didn't manage to make the Hajj.

The most important part of the Hajj is when pilgrims travel to the nearby Plain of Arafat where the Prophet Muhammad ﷺ preached his last sermon. Here, the pilgrims stand and pray in the heat from noon till sunset, asking God for forgiveness. Next they go back

towards Makkah, stopping at a place called Mina. Here they perform a ritual 'stoning of the devils'. Seven stones are thrown at three pillars in memory of how Ibrahim once rejected the devil. An animal is sacrificed and male pilgrims have their heads shaved. The pilgrims then return to Makkah to perform a further seven circuits of the Ka'bah.

▼ *A Muslim who has completed the Hajj is known as 'Hajji'. This home, in the village of El-Asasif in Egypt, has been decorated to show that its owner is a Hajji.*

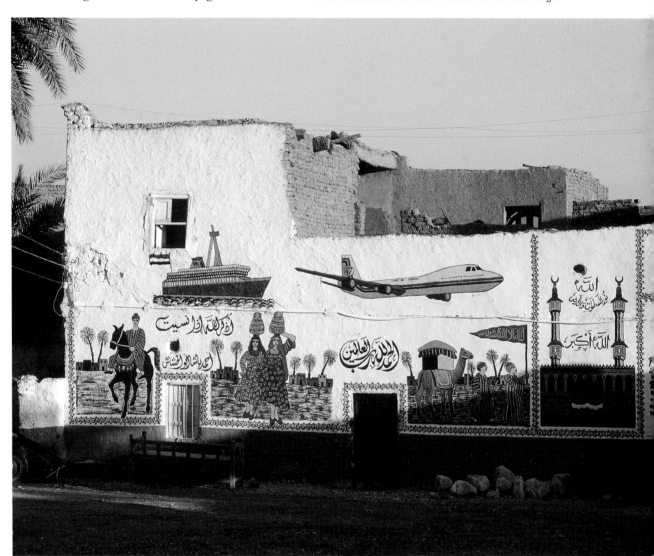

4 Living the faith

Being Muslim is not just about saying prayers, going to the mosque and feasting or fasting at special times. Being Muslim is a complete way of life – from birth to death. The Qur'an and the teachings of the Prophet tell a Muslim how to live each minute of each day.

Family life

For Muslims, the family is all-important. When Muslims become parents, they have a duty to see their children grow up understanding the faith. As soon as a baby is born, its father whispers into its ear the Shahadah: 'There is no god but God and Muhammad is his Prophet.' In this way, the very first words the baby hears are about God and his Prophet. By hearing these words the baby is welcomed into the

weblinks

For more information about Islam and life as Muslim, go to www.waylinks.co.uk/series/ 21stcentury/Islam

◄ *A father whispers the Shahadah into the ear of his new-born baby.*

faith. Naming a baby is also important. Sometimes the name of the Prophet or of one of his family is chosen, along with several family names.

Muslim children learn about their religion by watching their parents and following their example, for example seeing how they pray five times a day. Although Muslims may say these prayers wherever they are, the Prophet told his followers that they should say some of their prayers at home every day.

As Muslim children get older, they are expected to work hard at school and to help with the jobs at home. There are rules to guide Muslims when it comes to making friends and spending time outdoors. All teenagers are expected to show respect to older people because they have more experience of life than the young. Once they are grown-up, children are expected to care for their parents as they reach old age, in return for the care the children received when young. Muslims often live in large family groups and members of the whole family help each other at all times.

Family life is so important for Muslims that much of the home may be kept private from outsiders. Visitors will be shown to a guest room and will meet the men (and boys) of the family. The women (and girls) may stay in another room where they may receive their female guests.

Muslims also believe that all believers belong to the one family of Islam, whatever their skin colour, and that they should help those members of that family who are poorer than themselves by giving zakah (see page 36). Helping people may also take forms other than financial help.

▼ *A Muslim family in Hievlev, Denmark, come together to celebrate the end of Ramadan – the festival of Id-ul-Fitr (see page 28). Such family occasions are very important times in the Muslim year.*

Marriage

Marriage is very important to Muslims. To be regarded as a fully grown-up member of the family, a Muslim must usually be married. The Qur'an encourages all Muslims to marry and to have children.

In Arabia at the time of the Prophet, a man could have as many wives as he chose. The Qur'an changed this, saying that a man should have no more than four wives. If he did, it was his duty to treat them all equally. However, it has always been rare for a Muslim man to have more than one wife – partly because very few men could afford to keep two wives. But some Muslim men do marry a second wife if the first wife is unable to have children, or if she becomes too ill to look after the children. In Western countries, it is against the law for a Muslim to have more than one wife.

Before a Muslim wedding takes place, the couple agree rules for their marriage and these rules are written down, signed and witnessed as a contract between them. There is usually a wedding party about the time the couple begin to live together.

Divorce

Divorce is discouraged but is not forbidden if the marriage has completely failed. If divorce does happen, the wife receives some money from her ex-husband and keeps all their household goods. The husband then has no more responsibility to her. Re-marriage is allowed.

◀ *In Pakistan, a Muslim man and woman (wearing traditional dress) have become husband and wife in the presence of both families. Music and feasting will follow for the rest of the day and long into the night.*

Arranged marriages

For Muslims, a marriage means the joining not just of two people but of two families. For this reason, the choice of partner is seen as a matter of importance to the whole family and so Muslim marriages are often 'arranged' by parents and older relatives. It is often said that parents can see more clearly who would make a good life-long partner for their child than the young person. Most young Muslims are happy to follow their family's choice – but in the 21st century some young Muslims (especially those living in Western countries) want the right to make their own choices. Even where a wedding is 'arranged', a young person has the right to refuse the person chosen to be their partner. Islamic law forbids forced marriages.

◀ Not every Muslim couple wears traditional dress for their marriage ceremony. This Chinese couple have just married in Mongolia.

Zakah

Zakah (sometimes spelt zakat) is one of the 'pillars' of Islam (see page 21). It is the duty or obligation for all those who can afford it to give money (or food) to the poor and others in need. For example, money may be given to help those who have suffered from a disaster such as an earthquake, or to help with the building of a hospital or mosque – or to help a poor student to study at a college or university. The word 'zakah' means 'that which makes pure'.

Zakah is not something a Muslim chooses to do because he or she feels kind or generous – nor is it a tax. Muslims believe that, because everything in the world belongs to God, everything one owns really belongs to God. They also believe that God will judge how wisely each Muslim uses what he or she has been given. Giving 'zakah' reminds Muslims of this teaching.

There are complicated rules about how much zakah should be paid. Crops, herds of animals and deposits in banks count as part of a person's wealth. Homes, clothes and furniture do not. It is up to each Muslim to decide if he or she should pay more zakah than is necessary, but a minimum of 2.5% is payable. It is usually collected each year at the festival of Id-ul-Fitr, and is paid by women and children as well as men – if they have enough wealth.

▼ *At a mosque in Buckinghamshire, UK, two elders work out how the zakah should be distributed. In the centre is the imam of the mosque.*

The rich man and the poor man

Besides the religious duty of paying zakah, Muslims are also taught to be generous – as this story or parable shows:

'There was once a rich man and a poor man who owed him money. "Sir, I can't pay you what I owe," said the poor man, "but, if you give me time, I'll pay you when I can."

"Very well. Pay me when you can," replied the rich man.'

Islam teaches that this rich man will be rewarded by God for being kind. But the story goes on to show how much better it might have been:

'"Sir, I can't pay you what I owe," said the poor man, "but, if you give me time, I'll pay you when I can."

"You keep what little money you have," replied the rich man. "Forget what you owe me: it will be my zakah."'

▲ *Women in Fes, Morocco, meet together to learn and study the meaning of the Qur'an.*

Knowledge

The Prophet once said that it was the duty of every Muslim, male or female, to seek knowledge 'even as far away as China'. This pursuit to learn new things and to develop new inventions is known as *ilm*. It was once the main driving force of Muslim society and Muslims started the first universities, public libraries and public hospitals. The oldest university in the world opened in Cairo in Egypt in 970CE. Some Muslims, however, have interpreted ilm to mean only religious knowledge. When scholars have devoted themselves solely to the 'correct' interpretation of scripture, there has been a decline in scientific advance and in independent thought.

Mathematics

What are usually called Arabic numerals (1, 2, 3, and so on) originally came from India where they were developed by Hindu scholars. However, it was Muslim mathematicians who first invented decimals and developed the way we do basic arithmetic. Gradually, this system was passed on to the Western world which, until then, had used Roman numbers (I, II, III, IV and so on) which are more awkward to use in calculations. Not only did the West begin to use Arabic numerals, it also copied the Arabic system of reading or working traditional addition and subtraction sums from right to left (Arabic writing is read from right to left).

Muslim scholars invented essential branches of mathematics such as algebra, geometry and trigonometry, as well as bringing the number zero into use in mathematics (the concept of zero originally came from India).

◄ *This 16th-century painting shows Ottoman astronomers at the Galata observatory in Turkey, as they calculate the dimensions of the universe and the movements of the planets.*

➤ *The walls of the Wazir Khan mosque in Lahore in Pakistan are covered with decorated tilework, using geometric and floral patterns as well as beautiful calligraphy.*

Science

Five hundred years before anyone in the West, a Muslim astronomer called al-Biruni (973-1048) calculated the time it takes the earth to go round the sun (he was 24 seconds out), discovered the specific gravity of various metals and worked out that the earth rotates once a day. One of the greatest Muslim scientists was called al-Razi (died 925). He established midwifery, studied and wrote about eye disorders, measles and smallpox. Another Muslim scientist called Ibn Sina (980-1037; also known as Avicenna) wrote a 24-volume medical encyclopaedia which became the standard work of medical reference in both the Islamic and Western worlds for the next 700 years. Other areas of knowledge developed in the Muslim world included the science of optics, the use of oils for healing, veterinary science, town planning and underground mining. Muslim scholars also invented the compass, test tubes and surgical instruments, water mills and windmills – and the guitar.

Art

The Prophet taught that the worship of statues or idols is wrong, so the representation of living beings was strictly forbidden in mosques and other religious buildings, and in holy books such as the Qur'an. However, Muslim artists became experts in the creation of wonderful and intricate designs using flowers, plants and geometrical patterns, and these can be seen decorating the walls of mosques and other buildings the world over.

The skill of beautiful handwriting (known as calligraphy) is considered by Muslims to be the greatest form of art because it is used to write out words from the Qur'an. Words from the Qur'an in beautiful calligraphy have often been used as a surface decoration on the walls of mosques, on tiles, or on decorated pottery. The making of beautifully patterned cloth and decorated pottery (ceramics), metalwork, glass cutting and carving are all important forms of art in the Islamic world.

Death

Muslims try to ensure that nobody dies alone. When someone is dying, their family and friends gather round and ask forgiveness for any harm they have done. If possible, the dying person is reminded of the Shahadah (see page 20) – so the person dies as a believer. When death finally happens, the eyes of the dead person are closed and the body is washed by the family (a man's body by the men, a woman's by the women) and is then wrapped in white sheets. (The body of a person who has died in battle is not washed.)

In Muslim tradition, burial takes place on or as near to the day of death as possible. The body is taken on a stretcher to the mosque or straight to the burial place where prayers may be said by an imam. Burial is usually without a coffin so that the body will be in contact with the earth in which it is buried. The head is turned to face Makkah. Women do not usually attend the funeral, but visit the grave later. Muslims are never cremated.

Judgement

Islam teaches that each soul has its own separate identity. Muslims do not believe in reincarnation but in a 'Day of Judgement' when God will bring everyone back to life and decide how good or how bad each person has been. If the good things they have done are greater than the bad things, then an angel will lead them to Paradise. If the bad things are greater, then they will go to Hell. Muslims also believe that God is kind and merciful and that he will wipe out the bad things – provided the person is truly sorry for what they have done.

➤ *This 16th-century illustration shows the Mughal emperor Babur instructing his workmen about the planning of a new garden. The Qur'an says that Paradise is like a perfect garden, a place of peace and happiness. Many Muslim rulers have tried to design gardens similar to the ones in Paradise described in the Qur'an.*

◄ *A Muslim cemetery in Singapore. All Muslims are buried facing Makkah.*

In our own words

"When I die, I will be buried. Then the angels will ask me three questions. 'Do I believe in God?', 'Do I accept Muhammad ﷺ as his prophet?' and 'What is your book?' If I answer correctly, then I will wait until the Day of Judgement. As that's a long time, I'll be told my likely result on that day – whether I'll be going to Paradise or Hell."

5 Islam today

In the 21st century, Islam is seen by some people as being at war with the Western world and set against all the changes in modern life. Muslims themselves are divided as to whether Islam needs to become more 'modern' like, for example, some Gulf states such as Kuwait which are comparatively Westernized. In other countries (such as Saudi Arabia and Iran), Muslim tradition is strictly upheld.

Women in Islam

Islam teaches that men and women are equal but different. For example, politics is usually thought of as a job for men, while women must be responsible for the home and the family. But women have equal rights to own property and to be educated. They are allowed to take jobs outside the home – often working as teachers or in hospitals. This freedom varies from country to country. In Pakistan, a woman became Prime Minister.

In other Muslim countries, women are still not allowed to drive cars. Many Muslims now admit that women have not always had the dignity that the Qur'an teaches and have been denied their rights.

Dress

The Qur'an teaches that both 'men and women should lower their gaze and be mindful of their chastity' (Surah 24:30-31). This means that they should dress modestly. While men usually keep themselves covered at least from the navel to the knees, this rule has been taken to mean that women must be covered from head to foot, showing only their wrists, feet and face – and in some cases only their eyes. In many Muslim countries, this is being questioned by women who increasingly want greater freedom.

◄ *Benazir Bhutto was elected Prime Minister of Pakistan in 1988. She was the first female leader of a Muslim state.*

---
weblinks

For more information about Islam in the modern world, go to www.waylinks.co.uk/series/21stcentury/Islam

---

The hijab

The hijab is a veil that covers the head and shoulders. It is worn by some Muslim women, but not by others. Here, four Muslim women explain their choice:

"People think I'm forced to wear the hijab by my parents. I'm not. I want to wear it. It's a benefit. I have more confidence in myself. And people don't swear at me when I'm wearing it."

"We don't wear the hijab all the time. We don't wear it at home when there are just family members around. This is what the Qur'an says."

"The hijab frees you from everyone brainwashing you, you know, saying 'Buy this, buy that, you're supposed to look like this'. I don't have to worry about being popular by buying things that are 'cool'."

"I was born in Britain and I've just started working in a bank. I'm allowed to wear the hijab at work but I choose not to. I like the freedom and the chance to dress like the other girls at work."

▼ Turkey is a secular state in which the vast proportion of the population is Muslim. Some of the women in these groups gathered on the seafront in Istanbul wear the hijab; others wear Western dress.

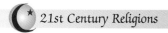

Conflict

On 11 September 2001, terrorists hijacked four planes and crashed two of them into the World Trade Center buildings in New York, USA, destroying the buildings and killing nearly three thousand people. A third plane crashed into and damaged the US Pentagon building in Washington D.C., but the terrorists in the fourth plane were overcome by the passengers, who crash-landed that plane in Pennsylvania, killing all on board. The terrorists were Muslims who were working for Al-Qaeda, a militant Islamic terrorist group. Since then, Islam and terrorism have often been linked. But as one Muslim said, "Those men were senseless. What they did was evil and very wrong. Islam was not to blame."

Islam teaches decency and care for all that God has created. It teaches that violence is wrong and that it is wrong to hurt the innocent. However, it also teaches that it is right to defend the faith when attacked – but only in self-defence.

Fundamentalism

Fundamentalists are people who believe that holy books (such as the Qur'an) are true in every word, cannot be altered, and are true today in the same way that they were when they were first written down. Fundamentalists often choose one part of a holy book and concentrate on that, forgetting other things written elsewhere in the book.

In the last thirty years, a number of Muslims have become very angry about what they believe is going wrong in the world. The result has been the rise of a modern fundamentalism: a desire to strengthen Islam by insisting on the 'purest' form of the religion. In practice, Muslim fundamentalism varies from country to country. In Iran, women may drive cars and go out to work, but under the fundamentalist Taleban regime in Afghanistan, women did not even have the right to a basic education. The aims of fundamentalists also vary. The Palestine resistance movement, Hamas, wants to create an Islamic republic in just one country. The leader of Al-Qaeda, Osama bin Laden, has expressed a desire for a united Islamic empire under central control. These ambitions may be political, but the movements are underpinned by support from religious fundamentalists.

◄ *A woman holds posters reading 'Implement shari'ah law' during a demonstration in Jakarta, Indonesia, in February 2004. The word shari'ah means the 'way' or 'path' to be followed by all Muslims. It has also come to mean 'a system of laws' to help Muslims follow this path, and is often used to describe the strict legal system in fundamentalist Muslim states.*

▲ In many places around the world, members of the different world faiths meet and work together to try to understand one another better. Here, Christians, Jews and Muslims gather for a Ramadan meal at the Islamic Center of America in Detroit, USA, in December 2001.

Looking ahead

For eight hundred years, Muslims led the world in science and learning, making new inventions, and in travel and in trade. Then the Muslim countries lost their power and were colonized or occupied by Western nations. Many Muslims are still angry about this and have tried to make Islam stronger by following the teachings of Islam more strictly. Other Muslims feel it was their own fault they lost power, and they are keen to build links with the West and to live according to the will of God – in peace with the rest of the world.

In our own words

"I'm proud to be Muslim. I cover my head, I grow a beard like all proper Muslim men should. I don't wear Western clothes and I've got satellite television so I need only watch Arabic programmes. My duty as a Muslim is to fight for God – even if he wants me to give up my life. What's wrong with that?"

Glossary

Allah The Arabic word for God.

ayatollah A leader of Shi'ah Muslims.

Bismillah The words that open every chapter of the Qur'an (except the ninth): 'In the name of Allah, the compassionate, the merciful'.

calligraphy The art of beautiful handwriting.

cremation The burning of a body after death.

crusade A medieval Christian war against Muslims.

Exordium The opening words of the Qur'an.

Hadith The sayings of the Prophet Muhammad ﷺ.

hafiz The title given to a person who has learned the Qur'an by heart.

Hajj The annual journey or pilgrimage to Makkah.

hijab A veil that covers the head and shoulders, worn by some Muslim women.

Hijrah The departure of the Prophet from Makkah for Yathrib (Madinah) in 622CE. This is the date from which Islamic years are counted.

id (eid) A festival.

idol A statue or image worshipped as a god.

iftar Food eaten at the end of the day's fast during Ramadan.

ilm The pursuit of knowledge and learning.

imam A Muslim (man) who leads prayers in a mosque.

Islam Means literally 'peace and submission' or 'obedience to God'.

Ka'bah The cube-like structure in the centre of the Great Mosque in Makkah. It was the first house built for the worship of the one true God.

khalifah ('successor') One of the early leaders of Islam.

mihrab An arch in a mosque, showing the direction of Makkah and the Ka'bah.

minaret The tall tower of a mosque.

mu'adhin (muezzin) A man who calls Muslims to prayer.

Mughals The rulers of a powerful Muslim Empire in India. Founded in 1526, it eventually came to an end in 1858.

Muslim A follower of Islam.

Ottomans Rulers of a powerful Muslim Empire based in present-day Turkey, with its capital at Istanbul. It lasted from about 1300 until 1920.

qiblah The direction in which Muslims face when praying, towards Makkah and the Ka'bah.

Qur'an ('recitation') The Muslim holy book, revealed to the Prophet Muhammad ﷺ.

Ramadan The ninth month of the Muslim year, during which Muslims fast during daylight hours.

rashidun The 'rightly guided ones'. The first four khalifahs, Abu Bakr, Umar, Uthman and Ali.

revelation A message from God.

salah (salat) Praying five times a day.

sawm Fasting from dawn to sunset during the month of Ramadan.

Shahadah The summary of the most important Muslim belief: 'There is no god but God and Muhammad is his Prophet'.

shari'ah The 'way' or 'path' followed by all Muslims, based on the Qur'an and the Sunnah.

Shi'ah Muslims who believe in the successorship of the fourth khalifah, Ali, after the Prophet Muhammad ﷺ and eleven other imams after Ali.

Sirah A written account of all the doings of the Prophet Muhammad ﷺ.

soul The inner, spirit-like part of a person, said to live for ever.

sufi Muslims who try to become close to God by leading very simple lives, and by using techniques such as chanting and dancing.

suhoor A light meal eaten before dawn during Ramadan.

Sunnah ('method' or 'example') The life, thoughts and sayings of the Prophet; the Hadith plus the Sirah.

Sunni Muslims who believe in the successorship of the rashidun, the first four khalifahs after the death of the Prophet Muhammad ﷺ.

surah A chapter of the Qur'an.

Taleban The fundamentalist Muslim government that controlled Afghanistan from 1995 until 2001.

tawhid The belief that there is one and only one true God.

wudu Washing before prayer, touching the Qur'an or entering a mosque.

zakah (zakat) An annual gift of money.

Timeline

CE

c.570	Birth of the Prophet Muhammad ﷺ
595	The Prophet marries Khadijah
610	The Prophet receives the first revelations from Angel Jibril
622	The Prophet makes the Hijrah to Madinah; Muslim calendar dates from this year
630	Muhammad ﷺ takes control of Makkah and throws idols out of the Ka'bah
632	Death of the Prophet; Abu Bakr becomes first khalifah
634-44	Umar is second khalifah
638	Muslims conquer Jerusalem
644-56	Uthman bin Affan is third khalifah
656-61	Ali bin Talib is fourth khalifah
690s	Dome of the Rock mosque completed in Jerusalem
732	By this date Muslim rule extends from Spain to India
762-66	Building of Baghdad, then the largest city on earth
1099	Christian crusaders conquer Jerusalem
1187	Muslims under Salah-ad-Din retake Jerusalem
1301	Founding of the Ottoman Empire
1501-1732	Safavid Empire
1520-66	Reign of Emperor Suleiman
1526	Founding of Mughal Empire
1857	British capture of Delhi, India
1858	End of the Mughal Empire
1918	Collapse of the Ottoman Empire
1926-32	Establishment of the united kingdom of Saudi Arabia
1947	British rule ends in India; the country is partitioned to form Muslim state of Pakistan
1964	Founding of the Palestine Liberation Organization
1967	Israel defeats Arabs in the Six Day War
1968	PLO turns to terrorism
1979	Establishment of the Islamic Republic of Iran
1982	President Sadat of Egypt assassinated by Islamic fundamentalists
1995-2001	Taleban rules Afghanistan
2001	Terrorist attacks on New York and Washington, USA

Further reading

Ideas of the Modern World: Fundamentalism by Alex Woolf (Hodder Wayland, 2003)

Introducing Islam by Ziauddin Sardar and Zafar Abbas Malik (Icon Books UK, Totem Books USA, 2001)

Religions of the World: Islam by Jamal J Elias (Routledge, 1999)

World Religions by David Self (Lion Publishing, 1996)

Index